Discover Volcanoes

by Victoria Marcos

D1527068

© 2014 by Victoria Marcos
ISBN: 9781623956394
eISBN: 9781623956462
ePib ISBN: 9781623956479
Images licensed from Fotolia.com

First Edition
Published in the United States by Xist Publishing
www.xistpublishing.com
PO Box 61593 Irvine, CA 92602

xist Publishing

A volcano is a mountain with a pool of melted rock below the surface of the earth.

3

When pressure builds up, the top of the mountain explodes.

Gases, rock and lava shoot up through the top of the volcano into the sky.

Molten (melted) rock is found at the center of the Earth.

When it comes out of a volcano it's called lava.

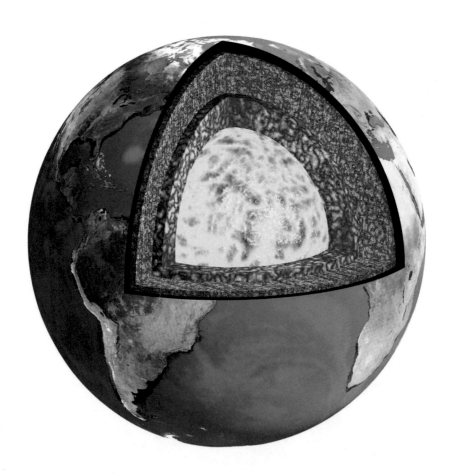

You can see how molten rock that is under the Earth shoots out from the top of the volcano.

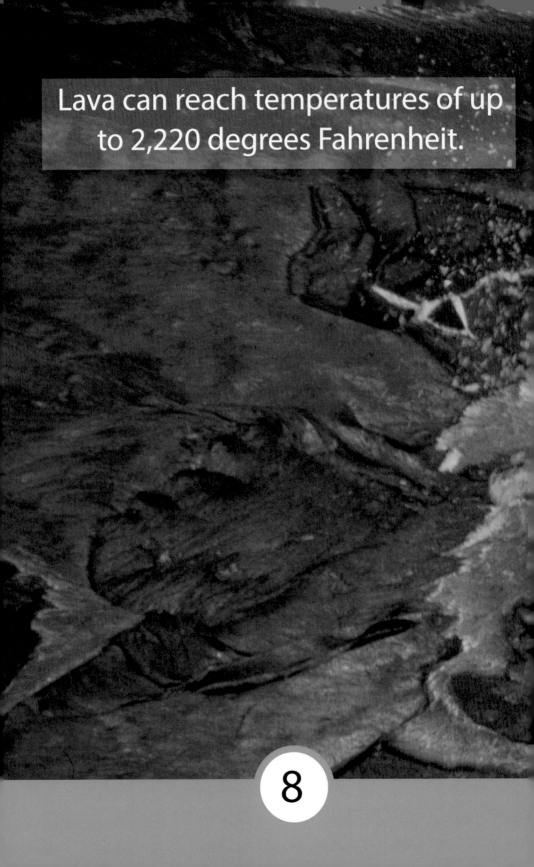

Lava can reach temperatures of up to 2,220 degrees Fahrenheit.

As the volcano erupts more and more, it gets bigger and bigger.

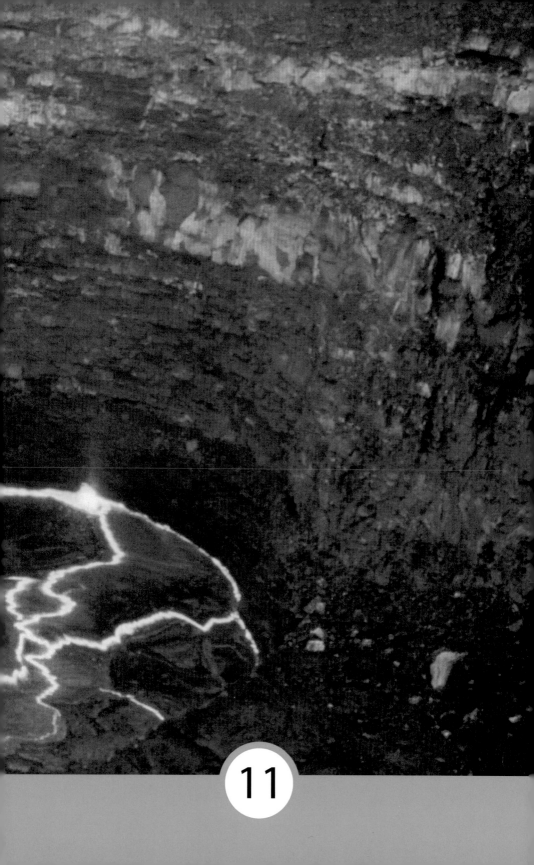

11

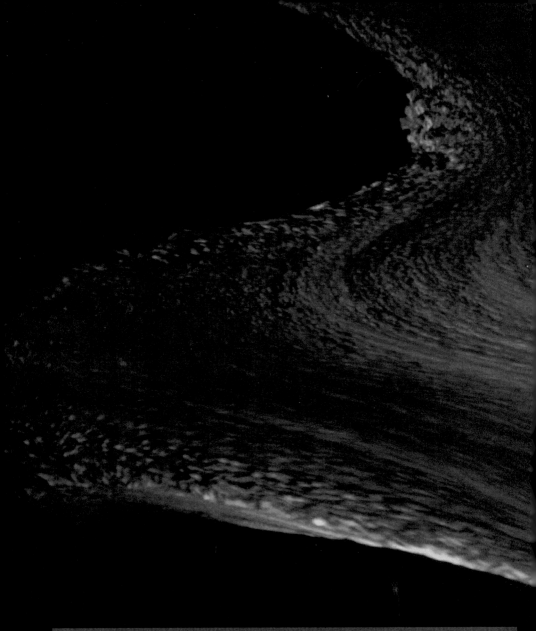

Lava flows out of a volcano
like a thick river.

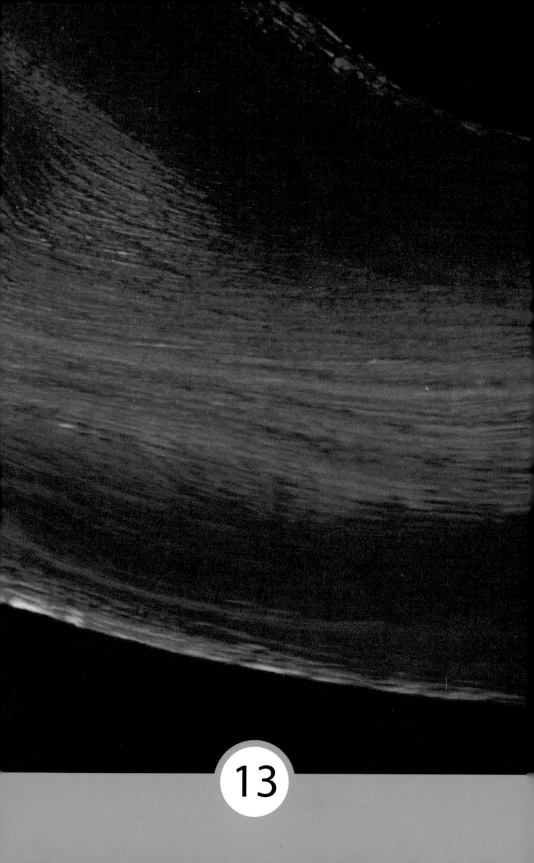

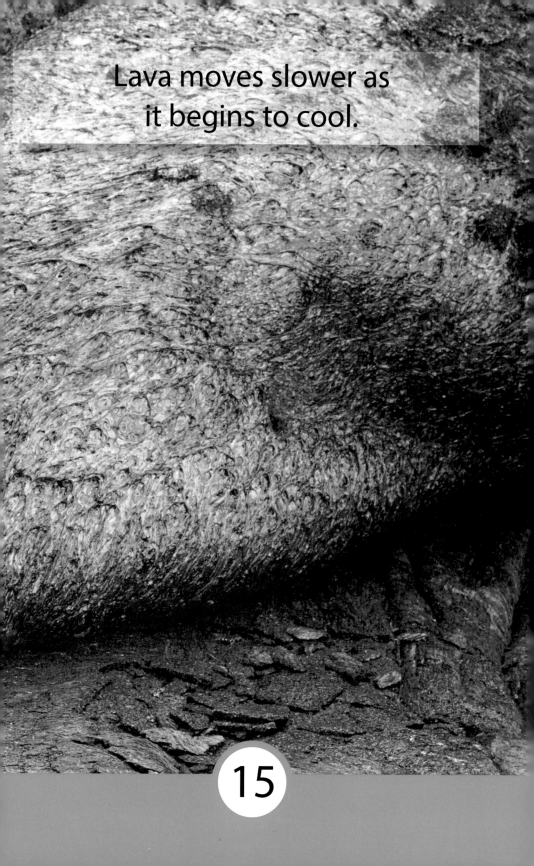

Lava moves slower as
it begins to cool.

When lava cools, it becomes a light, volcanic rock.

Volcanic rock is lighter
than other rocks.

19

Scientists that study volcanoes are called "volcanologists."

The study of volcanoes is called "volcanology."

Scientists wear special clothing to protect themselves from the heat of the volcano.

23

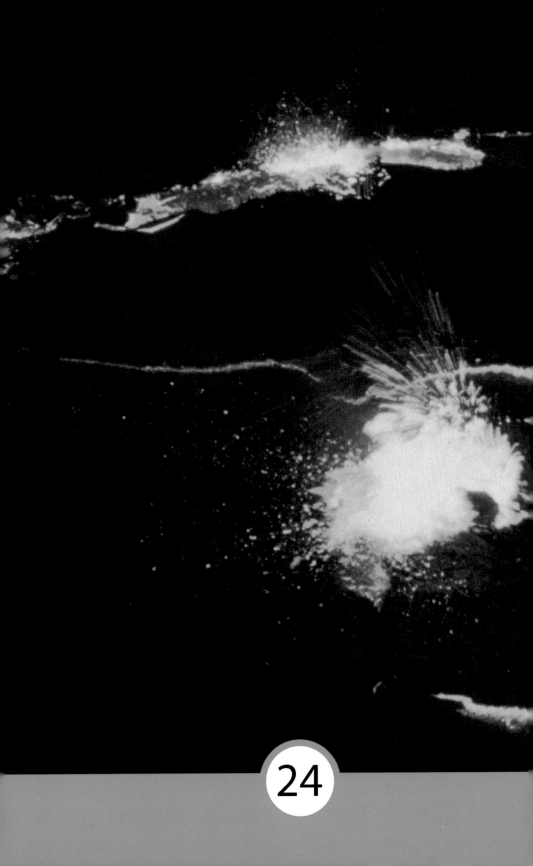

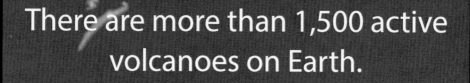
There are more than 1,500 active volcanoes on Earth.

More than 80 of them are
under the oceans.

26

Mt. Vesuvius in Pompeii, Italy is one
of the most famous volcanoes
in the world.

29

The Irazú Volcano is high up in the mountains of Costa Rica.

The Yellowstone Caldera shoots out hot water high into the air.

Lava can bubble and explode for hours and sometimes days.

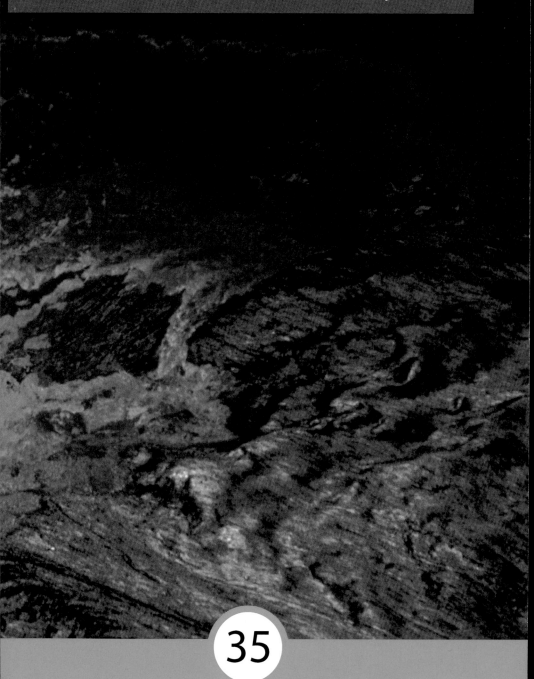

Made in the USA
Columbia, SC
23 February 2019